BORN *pierce*

BORN fierce

HOW TO UNLEASH THE CONFIDENT WOMAN WITHIN

TARIA PRITCHETT

Copyright © 2017 by Taria Pritchett

All rights reserved.

No part of this publication may be reproduced, distributed or transmitted in any form or by any means, including photocopying, recording, or other electronic or mechanical methods, without the prior written permission of the author, except in the case of brief quotations embodied in critical reviews and certain other non-commercial uses permitted by copyright law.

Manufactured in the United States of America.

Book Cover Design by Ana Grigoriu
Book Edited by: Darriel Tanner/Must Be the Pen
www.UnleashYourFIERCE.com

ISBN: 978-0-9986337-0-1 (pbk)
ISBN: 978-0-9986337-1-8 (ebk)

For print or media interviews with Taria,
Please contact taria@unleashyourfierce.com

DEDICATION

*To my mother, for loving me, supporting my vision,
and cultivating my gifts and talents;*

*to God, for making me into a highly valuable
and virtuous woman with purpose;*

*and to you, for allowing me to empower and serve you
on your journey to become
the FIERCE woman you were destined to be.*

DEFINING *FIERCE*

[FIERCE] Woman:

A woman who has found her FIERCE edge, Ignited her inner Queen, Elevated her confidence, Raised her men and money magnetism, Cultivated her sexiness, and can Empower herself daily effortlessly.

Synonyms: powerful, strong, fearless, confident, unstoppable

As you read, share your favorite quotables, snippets, and aha moments using the hash tag

#bornfierce

Also, since you are serious about becoming FIERCE since you brought this book, download your FREE companion workbook at:

www.unleashyourfierce.com/bookbonus

FIERCE MANIFESTO

I was born FIERCE.

I am worthy of winning.

My confidence, strength, and power comes from within.

I believe in myself.

I believe I am worthy.

I believe in the beauty of my dreams.

Heal. Evolve. Grow.

I am self-love in action.

I am purposed by design.

I know that confidence is everything.

I am bold, fearless, and confident.

I am unstoppable and unbothered by what others think.

I give myself permission to be great.

I own who I am flaws and all.

I am enough.

I am confident.

I am FIERCE.

I am committed deeply to myself.

I love who I am and the woman I am becoming.

I was born FIERCE!

CONTENTS

Introduction 11
PART I: HONOR YOUR CALLING
Chapter 1: The Journey to Evolve as a Woman 19
Chapter 2: Define Your Destiny 29
PART II: FORGIVE YOUR PAST
Chapter 3: Acknowledge Your Truth 41
Chapter 4: Heal Your Past 47
Chapter 5: Release Your Baggage 67
PART III: FALL IN LOVE WITH YOURSELF
Chapter 6: Become Confident & Empowered 81
Chapter 7: Step-Up Your Self-Love & Self-Worth 92
Chapter 8: Commit to Confidence Daily 105
Final FIERCE Thought: Step Into Your Power 115
EXCLUSIVE EMPOWERMENT EXTRAS
Book Bonuses 121
Book Club Guide 122
Appendix of Affirmations 124
Additional Resources 127
About Author 129

INTRODUCTION

"A woman in harmony with her spirit is like a river flowing. She goes where she will without pretense and arrives at her destination prepared to be herself."
- Maya Angelou

You know her. She is FIERCE. She is sophisticated. She is on the move. She is beautiful. Her beauty flows from her effortlessly. Her style is all her own. She simply glows.

Although on the outside she shines, there is just something about this woman that lights up an entire room when she enters. Her presence is radiant. Her spirit is peaceful, and her demeanor is happy.

She is loveable, and men want the chance to speak to her. Women even envy her or admire her. She is a purposeful woman, and it is evident she lives her life on purpose because she seems to have it all and has it all together. This woman is rare. She is one of a kind, and she is always sought after.

The reason why you know her so well is because as little girls, we deeply desired to be her. We want to be confident, regal, and beautiful. We desire to be love and be loved.

We yearn for a man who will protect us and provide for us. We long for happiness and joy. We put so much energy into dreaming about her, envying women like her, and underestimating our ability to be her that we don't even realize that we are already HER.

Every woman is born FIERCE!
All are called, but only few choose it.

So few women choose to be her because the process of **becoming** a woman of high value and virtue who glows with a sincere inner radiance and authentic confidence that comes from loving and accepting oneself wholeheartedly is NOT easy!

As much as the journey to self-fulfillment and personal empowerment is about becoming this kind of woman, it is even more so focused on you **unbecoming** everything that really isn't you so that you can become who you were really meant to be in the first place.

Consider the following:

- What would it look like for you to live an extraordinary life full of happiness, love, and abundance?

- How would it feel for you to glow and radiate confidence, self-love, and high value in every room you walked into?

- What would it mean for you to evolve yourself into the woman you desired to be, and you were able to finally live a life you love?

This book is your personal step-by-step guide to "unbecoming" and then becoming the woman you were destined to be and you desire to be. You were born to WIN. You were born to SHINE. You were born to glow. You were born to be FIERCE.

Now, you may not have been born with every single piece of wisdom and knowledge you needed to become the woman you desire to be, and that is fine. That is at no fault to you, honey. You have done the best that you have known how up until this point.

You may have failed. You may have made many mistakes. You may have made wrong choices. You may have made bad judgments. You may have believed false evidence appearing real (FEAR). You may have blamed others. You may have not forgiven people. You may be holding onto resentments, old agreements, toxic patterns, unhealthy memories, and even traumatizing incidents.

What I want you to know is that you are not alone. You don't have to go through anything in this life alone, and you don't have to go through any of it feeling bad for yourself. You also don't need to beat yourself up for any of it either.

Here is why:

> "I did then what I knew how to do. Now that I know better, I do better." – Maya Angelou

We are always operating from where we are. At any given moment, you do what you think is best at that moment. Whether it is good or bad does not matter. All that matters is that you recognize that your failures and mistakes don't define you.

Anything that lacks in your life doesn't define you. Anything that tries to hold you back doesn't define you. Anyone who has hurt you doesn't define you. Anything you've done that you aren't proud of doesn't define you.

These things also don't dictate your self-worth or value as a woman. Every experience is an opportunity to learn and to grow into your best self. When you know better, then and only then can you do better.

Sometimes we make the same mistakes over and over again, and we beat ourselves up about it, but like Margaret Thatcher once said, "You may have to fight a battle more than once to win it." This is truly the cornerstone of your evolution as a woman.

This book will serve as a tool that will enlighten you and help you do better, be better, and live better. In order to truly evolve and transform into a happy, healthy, healed, and whole woman, it is strongly recommended that you purchase a **beautiful journal** to house all the notes, exercises, and "aha" moments.

Born FIERCE is not just your personal guide, it is a journey that will touch you deep in your soul, heart, and mind in ways that you never would imagine. To be FIERCE, a woman must get to the root of all of the things that block her from loving herself fully, living a life she loves, and receiving the love she deserves.

The only true way to unleash your FIERCE is to not want everyone else around you to change, but for you to work on every issue you have within and unravel the beautifully and wonderfully made woman within yourself.

As we begin this journey together, I need you to know that this book is as much about you shining and thriving as it is about you getting down and dirty within what you are presented with. At times, I will challenge your thinking, belief systems, and ways of being. It may get a bit dark at times as you start to dig deep and get to the root of your personal struggles, fears, blocks, and issues.

However, "darkness always comes before dawn", and when you are on a journey of evolving into the woman you desire to be, you have to do the WORK to get to the other side! You can't evolve without going through the process of evolving. The process is real, raw, and honest. This is a process about recognizing your truth and owning that truth.

Throughout this process, please also note that at the heart of this journey is you recognizing and embracing your God-given strength, power, and talents. At the heart of all of my words and wisdom will be my own foundation rooted in God. Know that as a highly spiritual woman this will be embedded throughout this book and your journey.

I can guarantee you that if you trust in him and believe that he is guiding you to be an even better woman by way of reading my words, you will experience the most confident and fierce days of your life. I am here to empower you and challenge you to evolve into the woman you desire and were destined to be so you can live a life you love to live!

If you can open yourself up to experiencing one of the most amazing journeys of your life then let's begin!

– PART I –
∞
HONOR YOUR CALLING

Chapter 1

THE JOURNEY TO EVOLVE AS A WOMAN

There is no force equal to a woman determined to rise."
-   W.E.B. Dubois

It happened to me several times. I felt called to evolve as a woman and called to stretch myself and grow into the next level of being. My relationships nudged me, starting a business elbowed me often and went out and came back, and then all the weight I had lost and gained back prodded my mind. All of which is where I would find the deepest inkling to evolve as a woman, which in turn, had a domino effect on me changing my entire life...

We've all been there. We get intuitive hunches but disregard them. We get scared. We start to doubt ourselves. We brush it off and keep it moving. We get comfortable being content; however, we know deep down inside of us that we are not fully operating in our power.

I finally knew I had to get my shit together. However, we know we want better for ourselves. If only we knew how to get better and do better, we could be better. But we make excuses, we resist the process to becoming more fierce, we seek validation, and worst of all, we wait for permission to really take that step to the next level. So we remain stuck. We remain the same. We remain stagnant. We struggle with finding the way because we don't realize who we really are….

Little do we know, we were truly born to be FIERCE! You are truly worthy! You were born to win! You were born with a purpose! No one else can claim your space in the world. Since conception, you were born special, girl! No one else can say they have the same parents as you, were born on the same day at the same time, with your name, and with your DNA. Twins even have their own DNA!

When you took that first breath, history was made. The world can never be the same because you are here. Everybody doesn't make it here. But you did! Out of the 700 billion people in the world, you are unique. You are special. You are purposed. God didn't bring you this far to leave you now. You are here for a reason. Your life matters. What you can contribute to the world matters. You were beautifully and wonderfully made.

You are divine and one of a kind!
If you didn't know, now you know.

The confidence you crave and that empowerment you desire is yours! It is in you. It has always been in you. It is just waiting for you to unleash it! You don't have to look far to find it. Where you most need to look is within. The power lies within you. You have had it all along, darling!

This book will show you how to wake up and claim what's yours. Radiating with purpose, shining with self-love, and glowing with confidence is not for a select few of women. It is not for celebrities, so-called pretty girls, or even the very women you compare yourself to!

No, honey FIERCE is for you. It is your birthright.

Being FIERCE is a state of mind. It is a way of being. Your FIERCE is connected to all parts of your being. It is not something you turn off and on for certain people or certain occasions. It is a presence and an energy that needs to fill you every second of every minute of every day.

When your FIERCENESS is dull, you are operating from a very low vibration, and this is the type of energy that attracts negative experiences, unfulfilling opportunities, and even mediocre men. You can only attract what you are.

What I know for sure is that while I appeared to be FIERCE on the outside, there was much work that needed to be done on the inside. When one of my old beloveds announced to me that he had fathered a child while we were in a relationship, my whole world flipped upside down. I thought for sure I was in love, girl, and I was. But God had other plans for that relationship.

This sparked my evolution, and just one day after hearing that devastating news, I attended an African American leadership conference where I had the opportunity to hear actor, Courtney B. Vance speak as a keynote. He and his wife, the oh-so-fabulous and talented Angela Bassett, had just written and published a book entitled, *Friends: A Love Story*. This was just one day before I had received the news that really made me beyond depressed, to say the least.

So there I was, young and madly in love but heartbroken. I covered up my pain as I navigated this conference. As Courtney made mention of his wife, his face lit up into a vibrant glow of respect, pride, and love. As he continued to speak, two big screens on the side of his podium were moving a mile a minute with pictures of Mrs. Bassett. As the audience captured the pictures, he continued talking about how amazing she is, how much he loves her, how beautiful she is, how she's such an all-around confident woman, and why he is so proud to call her his wife.

This man was obviously in love, but what a great pitch to inspire the audience to buy his book. Boy, did he sell it. In that moment, he ignited the idea in me that a woman could be so powerful that her man would stand in front of a room of about three hundred people and boast of his wife's magnificence, beauty, and brilliance to the world!

With all the negative thoughts racing through my mind, this idea was like both a breath of fresh air and a wakeup call. It posed a few questions, and I began wondering, "Well what the heck am I doing wrong?" "How can a woman radiate in her purpose and power like that?" "How can a woman have such a loving, supportive and healthy relationship like that?" "How is it that she is able to have it all?"

Deep inside I was struggling like crazy trying to figure out how on earth I ended up in that situation, but something in me clicked about their love story. It was more so of the glow, strength, confidence, and power Angela had (and girlfriend wasn't even present at this event).

See when a woman got it going on, she doesn't even have to be in the room for people to feel her **FIERCE** energy! That moment resonated within me, and it has never left me. It occurred to me that being a confident woman, who radiated with purpose, was the new direction my life was headed from that point on. I made up my mind that I simply wouldn't ever let a relationship get to a point where I would receive that kind of disappointing news again!

At the moment, I was convinced that I was done with all things that no longer served and contributed to me wholeheartedly loving myself! It took me well over a year, maybe even two (don't judge me now!), okay maybe like four to leave, heal, and move on from that relationship. Then I began my journey to reclaiming my **FIERCE** back once and for all.

I made up my mind that I would go on a journey in discovering how to come into my own as a woman whom believes in herself, gets a good man and good love, achieves her dreams, gets the body she desires, and has all of her dreams come true. I looked around my family and community and realized that I wanted to contribute something to the world. I wanted to be an example. I wanted to do what few women would dare to do successfully:

Be their authentic self unapologetically and be damn good at it!

Every woman has her own set of morals and values that she lives by. However, a FIERCE woman as I discovered on this journey through experience, working with numerous women through my personal development company, coaching and being coached by successful women, doing research, attending seminars, watching videos, and reading book after book, is a woman who consciously adopts a new way of being in the world.

She thinks differently and follows empowering and self-loving habits daily that positions her to navigate the world confidently and successfully at all times. A confident and fierce woman is not born, she is made. She is conscious and creates her life daily by her actions and beliefs. In receiving all of that inspiration, I was determined to discover why some women seemed to be fierce and "have it all," while others didn't.

I began documenting what I discovered in blog posts which allowed me to build a following of women who were also interested in discovering the same thing. The more I posted, the more women shared with me how helpful it was. I became more invested in not only learning this for myself, but doing it for the purpose of helping other women. To no surprise, I fell in love with empowering other women.

Then it hit me one day. This is exactly where I am supposed to be. As a 7th grader, I had started my own book club at my house. I loved to read and write! Therefore, I got the brilliant ideas to start a book club and named it, "Reader's Inner Circle,", and then I thought about it some more and changed it to "Black Girls Have Power Book Club."

I asked a few of my friends at school if they were interested. I created an application and had girls sign up left and right. My mom ordered the books in bulk, and I created folders as well as activities to go along with each book. When they arrived, we enjoyed snacks and discussed the books using the exercises I created.

My favorite part was using the female characters life and choices as a vehicle for understanding ourselves within the context of our society. Years later, I would realize that this was part of my destiny as a woman, and hearing Courtney B. Vance discuss Angela Bassett with such pride reminded me that I was responsible for the choices I made as a woman.

The more I thought about it, I decided that I was finally ready to become the woman I was destined to be, and I was sick and tired of staying where I was. So I decided to commit myself into fully embracing this time in my life of growth, reflection, and healing. I decided I wanted to change more than I wanted to stay the same. I was ready to unleash the confident and fierce woman that I knew lived within me. It was then that I realized that I was worthy of winning at life!

I started by asking myself a few questions:

- *Who was I?*
- *What kind of woman did I want to be?*
- *What kind of wife and partner did I want to be?*

- *What purpose would I serve in the world?*
- *What would I contribute to the world?*

The process of evolving deeply had begun! I realized quickly that this was going to be a journey and not a one stop shop! I embraced it with full force no matter how uncomfortable it felt. It required me to stretch myself in ways I never imagined.

It required me digging deep below the surface to uncover things that held me back. It required moving through my comfort zone. It required opening myself up to new ideas and habits. It required really owning who I was regardless of what others might say. It required believing in myself no matter what. It required being fearless and focused.

The process of becoming who you were destined to be is not easy. This is why every woman we know does not appear FIERCE. This is why so many women stay where they are. If it were easy, then every woman would do it. It takes heart, perseverance, courage, and strength.

You were born to be FIERCE, honor yourself by honoring your calling. It is divine. It is for you! Own it! Claim it!

- TARIA PRITCHETT -

SELFIE CHECK

- What is sparking me to evolve into a more confident and fierce woman?

- What experiences in my life have brought me to this point?

- Am I committed to doing the work it takes to become who I was destined to be?

When I honor the calling of my greatness, I will begin to unleash the confident and fierce woman within myself. The longer I resist the journey, the longer I will remain where I am.

#bornfierce

Download your FREE workbook to complete the selfie checks at:
www.unleashyourfierce.com/fierceworkbook

Chapter 2

DEFINE YOUR DESTINY

"Look closely at the present you are constructing: it should look like the future you are dreaming."
– Alice Walker

A woman seeking empowerment must first get a super clear understanding of who she is, the life she wants to lead, and how she foresees it unfolding. Although a confident and fierce woman recognizes that she is being led by divine flow and timing, she is still responsible for creating a vision for her life and taking conscious action to see to it that it becomes a reality.

Where you currently are in your life is what you have envisioned before. Most women don't want to take responsibility for their current state of being because it feels too icky to accept that they are the ones responsible for their current life circumstances.

Don't get me wrong—your childhood, relationships, and unexpected situations affect you. However, at the end of the day, your life is a reflection of your previous thoughts and beliefs. Not long after I began my journey of healing and evolving into the woman I desired to be, I slowly but surely increased my level of self-love, supercharged my confidence, and ignited my personal power in ways that I didn't even realize I could.

The most amazing part about this is that the journey was easier once I defined my destiny through writing, meditating, affirming, and visualizing.

A FIERCE woman stays empowered and connected to her destiny in five key ways on a daily basis:

1. Meditation

2. Visualization

3. Journalization

4. Affirmation

5. Activation

Meditation is a practice in which an individual trains the mind or induces a mode of consciousness, either to realize some benefit or as an end in itself.

Visualization is the practice of mentally envisioning the dreams and goals as if they have already happened or are happening in one's life.

Journalization is the practice of using a journal and writing for healing, evolving, and manifesting one's desires.

Affirmation is the act of affirming one self.

Activation is the practice of doing and being the desired outcome one wishes to foresee in their lives on a daily basis.

Most women automatically resort to reciting affirmations to aid them in becoming who they desire to be. They also create vision boards of the life they desire to have; however, women often times complain that they try it, but nothing changes. They are not growing or transforming in anyway. This is because the process of becoming the woman you desire to be requires that you constantly and consciously practice a combination of daily time-tested rituals that bring you clarity, focus, and direction.

Creating a vision board and saying affirmations will not change your life. However, journaling about your goals, writing down your dreams on paper, then creating a visual board to review daily, meditating on your vision, affirming your vision every morning, and then taking constant action towards making your vision a reality will produce the desired results. Once you do all of those things, you still might not see your vision come to fruition if you refuse to heal and get rid of anything that blocks your blessings from coming to you.

For example, you can make your affirmations and create vision boards for your ideal man and relationship to show up, but if you never heal from your past relationship drama and evolve into the type of woman who can attract the type of man you so desire, it won't happen!

On the journey to becoming confident and fierce, no part of your life is in isolation from the others. Your inner and outer life work together. Your outside reflects your inside, and your outer reality is a result of inner thoughts. All your thoughts affect each and every word you say, actions you take, people you associate with, clothes you wear, income level you have, places you work, relationships you attract, food that you eat, and so on.

Again, who you are is a result of who you believe yourself to be. Empowering yourself requires you as a woman to become more self-aware of who you are and where you see yourself going. You are less likely to get lost in other things (food—emotional eating ring a bell!), men, career, friends, TV, social media, etc.) or compare yourself to others when you are self-aware, confident, and fierce.

When a woman is destiny driven, she is living her life purposefully, and everything begins to fall into place. When I chose to heal, awaken, and gain clarity about my destiny, everything changed. The steps I took elevated me deep within and eventually reflected on the outside. I discovered my purpose and how to use my God given strengths and talents to the best of my ability.

I broke my tie to emotional eating and the weight loss-gain rollercoaster rides, and I became more productive, disciplined, and focused, which did wonders for my life and business. My income increased, and I revamped my business to gain more impact. I attracted new, like-minded women into my friendship circle and men who were more suitable and compatible for me.

It would be great if all you had to do was say an affirmation and boom, confidence fills you! However, it isn't that simple. You see... Where you are right now in your life reflects the energy that you embody within. Your energy is connected to your vibration. Your vibration is your aura. Your aura is your spirit. Your spirit is your foundation. Evolving this aspect of yourself requires a mindset shift which turns into an energy upgrade and then a lifestyle makeover.

For example, ever wonder why some women make millions of dollars while others struggle and live pay check to pay check? The millionaire has shifted her energy when it comes to money and now has a millionaire mindset because she now believes she is abundant and prosperous.

Whereas the other woman living paycheck to paycheck, is operating from a very low energy of lack thinking. She operates from a poverty mindset and believes money is scarce. No matter how many affirmations or vision boards the lady with lack thinking creates, she will never increase her income if she doesn't make a conscious effort to shift her energy around money. Even making more money won't change her financial status if she doesn't shift her energy.

This is true for every area in life not just money! So as you begin the process of declaring your destiny and what you desire for yourself and your life, complete a thorough examination of your life and where you want to go.

Your energy will determine your reality!
Your thoughts will dictate your destiny!

Here is a simple 5 step process to aid you on this journey....

Meditating: Meditating contributes to high level vibrational energy and aids in shifting. Lie down or sit with your back straight up. Quiet your mind. This takes practice. It may not happen on your first attempt. Savor the silence. Become aware of your breaths. Become comfortable with this newfound quiet space.

As you breathe in and out, release negative energy and emotions and welcome in peaceful and loving energy and emotions. In this space, you are opening the way to hear your inner voice, listen to a higher power, and manifest what you desire. Use this time to talk to yourself openly and honestly, ask God questions, and begin the process of visualizing.

Visualizing: Visualizing conditions your mind and spirit for new things to come into your life. In a state of meditation, begin to see what you desire for yourself and your life. Imagine yourself living up to your highest potential in which you feel most confident and fierce. Use all of your senses and see into your visions as if they are happening in the moment.

Journaling: Journaling solidifies your desires and increases the likelihood of it coming to fruition. Write down everything you visualize. Write down your goals. Write down your dreams.

Answer the following in your journal, with the assumption that the "ideal woman" is you:

1. The woman I imagined myself to be as a little girl was…

2. I want to be the kind of woman who…

3. It is important to me as a woman that I….

4. I want to interact with men in a way that…

5. Other woman and me….

6. Describe your ideal woman in five adjectives

7. What does being FIERCE look and feel like to you?

8. What does your ideal woman enjoy?

9. What does you ideal woman not enjoy?

10. What does your ideal woman do for a living?

11. What does your ideal woman look like?

12. How does your ideal woman feel on the inside most of the time?

13. What is your ideal woman good at?

14. What are your ideal woman's strengths?

15. What makes your ideal woman's life fulfilling and happy?

Affirming: Affirming establishes new standards of being, thinking, and living. Begin to affirm yourself daily by setting intentions about yourself and your life. If you intend to be more confident, outspoken, and self-loving, then create an affirmation that speaks to this.

For example,

*"I am confident and empowered. I am assertive, and I speak with authority.
I am in total, head over heels in love with myself, and I love my life."*

Your affirmations should reflect the woman you want to become. They must also be said consistently and daily for best results. Repeated actions become our habits. It takes 21 days to form a new habit. As we know habits are hard to break; therefore, starting a positive habit is worth it.

Please refer to the Appendix of Affirmations at the end of this book for more ideas.

Activating: Activating ignites opportunities and miracles to manifest. Your vision will never manifest without you doing the "work" it takes on the inside first and then the outside to see to it that you live your best life.

Your vision will begin to unfold….

The universe will begin to deliver…

God will release more of your blessings…

Only when you become the type of woman who is ready for the next step and realize that it is her time to shine and glow, will you see your life change. When you feel ready, simply begin speaking it into existence by saying, "It's my time, and I am ready for the next level. I am ready to leap into my destiny." Then create a list of actions you can take to reflect your goals, desires, and intentions.

Your life will change when your energy changes. When you operate from a higher vibrational frequency of abundance, prosperity, love, wholeness, health, wellness, and so on, you can call into your life things that match what you desire. Being FIERCE is the highest vibration. It is radiance. It is shine. It is strength. It is confidence. It is power.

Until you raise it, you will block some of your blessings, and not fully fulfill your potential. When you are in FIERCE mode, more good can flow into your life!

SELFIE CHECK

- How have my thoughts impacted me and my life up until now?

- In what areas of my life, could I use a shift in energy?

- What actions will I take to become the "ideal woman" I desire to be?

---

*My life is a reflection of my beliefs.
If I shift my energy, I can radiate auras of confidence and not contentment, prosperity and not poverty, beauty and not brokenness, worthiness and not worthlessness, and empowerment and not emptiness.*

#bornfierce

---

*Download your FREE workbook to complete the selfie checks at:
www.unleashyourfierce.com/fierceworkbook*

– PART II –
∞
FORGIVE YOUR PAST

Chapter 3

ACKNOWLEDGE YOUR TRUTH

"Until you heal the wounds of your past, you are going to bleed. You can bandage the bleeding with food, with alcohol, with drugs, with work, with cigarettes, with sex, but eventually, it will all ooze through and stain your life. You must find the strength to open the wounds, stick your hands inside, pull out the core of the pain that is holding you in your past, the memories and make peace with them."
— *Iyanla Vanzant*

Once you commit to shifting your energy, upgrading your aura, and raising your FIERCE vibration, you then need to acknowledge your TRUTH.

The truth is at the root of why you are not where you would like to be. When we begin to "OWN' our truth, then we begin to get what we want from life and love. The more we stuff it down, mask it, put band aids on it, and even cover it with bad habits such as emotional eating, negative thinking, sabotaging yourself, or even attracting men of low value and relationships birthed out of our desperate need to feel loved, the more we silently suffer in unworthiness, unlovable-ness, and invaluable-ness.

The longer we remain stagnant and make no progress towards living a life we love and having the love we deserve, we cannot become what we want on the surface without handling what is below the surface.

You must identify the unconscious beliefs and thoughts that are running your life at this moment. These can range from your insecurities, to your fears, to feelings of unworthiness, to why you lack boundaries to why the same things keep happening to you. Once these items are brought to the surface, you must deal with them in order to heal them and clear the way for new beginnings.

This process also requires my favorite "f" word: forgiveness.

The Art of Forgiveness

In order for a woman to evolve herself mentally, emotionally, physically, spiritually, sensually, and sexually, she must learn how to "let go." There is an art to forgiveness. Not only must we forgive others, but we must also forgive ourselves.

Forgiving ourselves frees us from the need to blame others and make others wrong. Forgiving ourselves also frees us from the need to house anger, worry, pain, resentment, fear, and jealousy within us. When we hold things in, they show up in our lives in other unhealthy ways such as through illnesses, disease, nasty attitudes, and negative energy that no one wants to be around.

If we are clouded with these unhealthy energies, we will never become FIERCE because our light and love for ourselves will be dimmed by those things we fail to "let go" of.

As Oprah Winfrey says, "True forgiveness is being able to say, "thank you for that experience". You will truly know if you have let go and forgave if you can acknowledge whatever the person or situation is, and value the experience you gained from it. As long as you hold on to it, it has power over you, and you will never evolve into the confident and fierce woman you desire to be.

It also important to recognize that forgiving someone does not mean the other party is "off the hook" or you forget totally what happened. Forgiveness is simply a way for you to free yourself of the negative effects of holding onto the negative energy and experiences surrounding a particular person or event.

Healing Exercise:

Create a list of all the people (including yourself) and experiences that you need to FORGIVE. Please note that the next chapter focuses entirely on your parents and childhood. Once the list is complete, read through each name aloud, forgive them, and then forgive yourself.

Once you have made it through the entire list, either shred or burn the paper and declare,

> "I am ready to heal. I forgive [insert each name on the list]. Wherever [insert each name] is I asked that he/she be blessed. I also forgive myself. Now that I know better, I will do better. I am ready to reclaim my power and unleash the fierce woman within me."

Self-Forgiveness Exercise:

Once this is complete, I encourage you to consider all of the things you need to forgive yourself for. Be honest and specific. This exercise is inspired by Colin Tippings' Radical Forgiveness method which is truly powerful and life changing. Answer the following questions in your journal to practice deep self-loving self-forgiveness:

1. What am I upset with myself for? Why?

2. I feel… (list your emotions) …..towards myself

3. I feel responsible because….

4. Now I take full responsibility for feeling…. and believing….and I am willing to let go.

Write and Speak Aloud

I now accept that what I was feeling is not a mistake. I now accept that what I experienced is not my fault. Wherever I am in my life is exactly where I am supposed to be. I now see that this situation is reflecting a part of myself that wants to heal, evolve, and grow— even if I don't know why. I am not at fault, and I will let go of those feelings. I now see this situation as a wake-up call to move me closer to become the woman I was destined to be.

*In this moment, I choose to forgive_____
_____ (your full name), love myself, and accept myself unconditionally. I let go of all of the negative emotions surrounding this situation. I take back my power. I reclaim myself at this time. I acknowledge that I create my life, and I choose to surrender this to God and divine flow.*

Follow this exercise with journaling how you now feel and visualize your life healed and whole. You must understand that carrying baggage decreases your vibrational energy and clouds your aura.

Truth be told: You deserve better! Your days of "bootleg happiness" are over! So, handle it before it blocks your blessings! You were not born to suffer, struggle, or settle as a "bag lady" in the words of Erykah Badu. You were born FIERCE!

SELFIE CHECK

- Who do I need to forgive? Why?
- What do I need to forgive myself for?
- How will I continue to practice forgiveness moving forward?

---

*Forgiveness is the gateway to healing.
Forgiving myself and others is
an act of self-love.*

#bornfierce

Download your FREE workbook to complete the selfie checks and forgiveness exercise at:
www.unleashyourfierce.com/fierceworkbook

Chapter 4

HEAL YOUR PAST

"Children have never been very good at listening to their elders, but they have never failed to imitate them."
— *James Baldwin*

Not only do we hold on to past hurts and pains and refuse to "let them go.", but we often unconsciously live our lives and build our relationships with ourselves and others based on our parents. Whether they were great or deadbeat, present or distant, loving or abusive, they have had an impact on the women we have grown to be.

We all have expectations of what our parents should have been like, and we all have our own recollections of what it was like from our perspectives. Rarely do we ever put ourselves in their shoes to better understand their choices and style of child-rearing. Sometimes we fail to realize that our parents are human and imperfect just like us.

One of the major blocks to FIERCENESS for all women is their inability to recognize that there are unconscious factors influencing their belief systems, lifestyles, and even their selections of men and friends. These unconscious factors are a direct result of your childhood. Whatever is experienced during childhood but is never dealt with, is called having a "childhood wound."

All people have childhood wounds, and each of us also have a mother wound and a father wound that need to be healed within us before we can fully awaken to our personal power and radiate in all of our feminine glory.

Healing Your Childhood Wounds

My mother always reminds me that "little people become big people," meaning what a child learns and sees in their household will always follow them no matter how old they become, and no matter how uplifting or damaging.

By the time we reach adulthood, everyone assumes that all of your past issues and pains will magically dissolve, go away, or shouldn't influence how a person thinks or behaves. Some people go as far as stuffing it down or acting as if they don't care.

I know because I was very good at that, especially when it came to my own father. He had stopped talking to me shortly after my 21st birthday, and he would never answer when I called. I stopped calling, and I resorted to an "I don't care attitude" and just told myself "he would be the one missing out."

However, four years later I soon realized that when I finally decided to heal that part of me, I didn't mean it at all. It was just a coping mechanism to hide my real pain, resentment, anger, and my growing belief that perhaps I wasn't "loveable, worthy, or important" enough for my father to reach out to me or call me in almost 4 years.

As a child, I loved my father! He always seemed more like me than my mom, although she primarily raised me. Whenever we actually did get together, it was always a good time. We shared conversation and meals at our favorite restaurants. We also enjoyed outings here and there. When Valentine's Day rolled around, he would bring me a gift to remind me that he was the only man I should be focused on until I was old enough for dating.

Sometimes he would randomly bring me books because he knew I loved to read, and other times he would call just to see how I was doing. My mom always reminded me that I was very similar to my dad, personality wise.

Consequently, I think that is why he and I connected so well. Despite his great qualities and our great connection, I deep down wished that I could share more time and conversation with him than I had gotten. Those times we did share were about once a month or every few months, and phone calls were every few weeks or so.

When I was around 5 years old, my mother and father broke up. I freaked. At the time, I didn't understand why he had to go away or why he was going to be with another woman. I wanted him to be at my house, and doing homework with me and talking with me. I wanted to be daddy's little princess and come home to see he had cooked. I wanted to see his face daily. Was that too much to ask for?

Shortly after, I got the grand idea to run away from home. I had no idea where I was going, but I just knew I had to get away. Unfortunately, I blamed my mother for his leaving, although it was in no way her fault. But, my five year old self did not understand, and I ran away.

We lived in a condo. I ran around the block in my little jean dress and ponytails. I didn't get far. Eventually, I came back home to find my mother very upset. She decided to take me to therapy so that I could work through my feelings of sadness and anger. All I remember doing is drawing pictures of myself, my mom with her black purse, and my dad. I desired to have the whole family back together. What little girl wouldn't? So I held onto those feelings until I couldn't anymore.

One day as I sat at my desk to teach, it all hit me. I thought it was healed during the therapy session, but it wasn't. As an English teacher, I had been teaching Harper Lee's *To Kill A Mockingbird*, and my students warm up was to analyze a quote. This particular day, one of my students had selected a quote regarding the characters in the book.

For those unfamiliar with the book, the story is set in a fictional town down south during the 1930's and revolves around the narrator and main character's father taking on a controversial case in which he defends a black man on trial for a crime he did not commit.

The quote by Sigmund Freud for that particular day was, "I cannot think of any need in childhood as strong as the need for a father's protection." I always have my students reword the quote of the day into their own words, agree or disagree with the quote, and then identify the members of society who would benefit the most from hearing the quote.

Lastly, I would ask students to share their responses. On this day, a variety of students shared, but two stood out to me that caused me to reconsider my relationship with my own father. There were two African American girls who shared and unlike their mostly white peers, I could feel their pain coming through their words. They both explained that they believed "dead beat fathers" could benefit from this quote because they would begin to understand the power of their presence and protection in their child's life.

Once they left that day, something inside me kept gnawing at their words. Although my dad was by no means a dead beat, something about those girl's responses triggered something deep in me. I went immediately to my computer to see what, if any, support I could find to help me make sense of all of these emotions that I didn't even know I harbored.

What I discovered was that there was resentment, anger, sadness, and hurt revolving around my relationship with my father that I had yet to handle. I had left it in the past and kept going as if nothing ever happened. I know I am not the only one who does this. It is easier to keep going. It is easier to drown yourself in your career, volunteer opportunities, men, social media, or something else in order to keep yourself so "busy" that you have no time to yourself.

The truth is that when you are alone, your thoughts are the loudest. Many of us are scared to hear what is really inside of ourselves. Many of us are scared to listen to the real truth that it is in our hearts, mind, and spirits. We fear what we might hear about ourselves. If it is anything less than perfection, we don't want to hear it. We think it is something wrong with us. We think we are "weird" or "unloveable", or unworthy" or "unimportant" or "unworthy" or even "unattractive."

It is not that you are any of those things. However, if you don't heal your past, then you will make it harder for you and others to fully love you, value you, honor you, cherish you, and make you important.

If you have ever watched even one episode of Iyanla's show, *Fix My Life* on Oprah's OWN network, you will see exactly what I mean. Iyanla can't go an episode without getting to the root as to why people's lives are where they are. More times than not, she can trace something back to someone's childhood that plays a major role in their thinking and behavior in this present day.

Our first few years on Earth matters more than you know. It lays the foundation for the woman you are to become. Who you are in this moment is who you were built to be from your childhood. Healing any unresolved issues that are still lingering would be beneficial not only to you, but all others in your life as well.

There is a peace and joy that comes with dropping baggage, as we all know.

Healing Any Mama Drama

Your mother has a very strong connection to you as she was the one who carried you for 9 months in her womb and gave birth to your being. You are deeply connected to her even if she abandons, abuses or rejects you.

In our society, the mother/daughter relationship is often discussed less than the father/daughter relationship and its impact on us as women. Mother/daughter relationships vary and are complex depending on the pair.

However, every woman has been influenced by her mother both positively and negatively. In fact, according to family therapist, Dr. Stephan Poulter, only 10% of people have a "complete" mother who was well balanced, nurturing, protective, and empowered their children to be an individual. He recognized that this "complete" mother was not perfect but gave her best despite it all.

For women with very strong and healthy mother/daughter relationships, they should still work on improvement because there is still room to heal and grow. For women with more challenging mother/daughter relationships, they should work on resolving these issues through deeper healing.

Regardless of the positive, negative, or somewhere in- between relationship you had with your mother, there is a "mother wound" inside of yourself that needs to be healed in order to master your own confidence and unleash your personal power.

This process is not about making your mother wrong, blaming her for who you are, or even trying to change her to be more of what you want. This is for you. It is about your acknowledging the truth about your mother and healing any parts that prevent you from being FIERCE.

Nonetheless, this is also about recognizing the parts your mother instilled in you that contribute positively to the woman you are and are becoming. It is also about you recognizing that your mother is (or was) a woman just like you.

Becoming a mother is one of the hardest yet most rewarding undertakings in a lifetime. It isn't easy. It also doesn't mean that your mother is perfect because quite frankly, she might have never mastered confidence, life, and love or unleashing her own FIERCE as a woman before you were born or during your childhood.

Even now it is unfair to expect your mother to have been "perfect." She is a human being just like you—flawed. In a society that pressures mothers and even women to be perfect in every single aspect of their lives all of the time, it is wrong to point fingers at our mothers for being less than perfect.

Not only that, but what about the parts of our mothers that have been passed down through generations—the good, the bad, and the ugly. Then consider the generational cycles, curses, and blessings that you are still carrying from all of the women in your family that came before you?

Acknowledging and healing your mother-wound is an excellent opportunity to break any karmic ties and bring healing to a familial pattern that may not serve you or future women to come in your family.

Before moving forward, reflect and identify what type of mother you had/have.

She can fall into more than one category, or she can have characteristics in different categories (circle them):

Hard Working Mother	Narcissist Mother	Absent Mother	Over-Involved Mother
-Very driven and focused career woman as your mother -Great role model for you -More mature and independent than peers -Sometimes felt unimportant and unseen -Often seeking attention from others	-Everything is about her -She is unable to empathize with you -Frequently want mother's attention and approval -Mother is often jealous of you -Often feel like "you're not enough"	-Distant, unavailable, or incapable of being fully present -Often feel resentment or anger toward her -Often feel unseen and unheard and unloved	-Struggle with boundaries - Live vicariously through you - Very critical and judgmental of you -You have strong desire for privacy and freedom - Really want to make her proud and want approval

Perfectionist Mother	Best-Friend Mother	Abusive Mother	Complete Mother
-Deeply desired to have it all and worked hard to have it	-Treats you more like a friend or a sister	-Emotionally, mentally, or physically abused by mother	-Wanted to and did her best to raise you despite life's circumstances
-Mother was competitive and often trying to keep up with other families or households	-Experienced very adult conversations with mother as a child	-Her words or actions cut you deeply	-Accepted you for your own uniqueness and help hone who you really are
-May have felt like you were lacking something and weren't good enough	-Hangs out with you and you hang out with her/her friends	-Mother could have possibly experienced substance abuse/physical abuse of her own	-Mother was emotionally balanced
-Could/can feel mothers disappointment or unhappiness with your decisions, actions, or feelings	-Have fun with mom, in some cases this mother can be irresponsible	-More likely to experience depression or feel unworthy	-You feel comfortable sharing with her and being your complete total self
	-You positively support your mother emotional needs	-Emotions and heart are more on guard with others	
	-Often feel	-May carry this into new	

-Inspired you to internalize perfection to some degree -Often become an overachiever in your own life	guilty or responsible for mother's well being	relationships; possibility you abuse others or others abuse you	

Mother Reflection: Based on the above reflections, which one(s) resonated with you the most, and if none of these fit, create your own description in your journal of your mother.

Be honest. Be specific. Tell the truth. Don't be afraid to point out praise as well as points of pain. Our job is to forgive our mothers and ourselves, love our mothers, and step into our own power and be great!

Bethany Webster exclusively researches and writes on the topic of mother wounds after healing her own wounds. On her website, *Womb of Light,* she addresses specifically why it is crucial for women to heal their mother wound.

She also shares the pain the mother wound causes and the ways it manifests in our everyday lives when it goes unresolved:

Pain the Mother Wound Causes	Ways an Unresolved Mother Wound Manifests In Everyday Life
-Feel not good enough -Consistently feel like something is wrong with you -Feel like you must remain small to receive love -Guilt for wanting more than you have	-Not being your full self because you don't want to threaten others -Having a high tolerance for poor treatment from others -Emotional care-taking -Feeling competitive with other women -Self-sabotage -Being overly rigid -Conditions such as eating disorders, depression and addictions and dominating

As grown women, it is imperative that we reflect on our relationships with our mothers.

Reflect and respond to the questions in a journal below:

1. How would you describe your mother/daughter relationship from birth to now?

2. The mothering I received as a child was....because....

3. How are you and your mother similar? different?

4. What are some things you loved about your mother growing up? Explain.

5. What are some things you disliked about your mother growing up? Explain.

After reflecting, there is a simple six step process you can take to overcome any feelings that came up that were not pleasant.

These steps are as follows:

1. **Reconnect with your younger self** by finding a younger picture of yourself and speak to her as if you were her mother.

2. **Understand how society sets up the idea of "motherhood" and its effects.** Reflect on your beliefs regarding motherhood versus what your mother's perceptions of motherhood may have been.

3. **Forgive your mother.** Write a letter to your mother in which you express all of your new found wisdom and insight regarding your mother/daughter relationship. Forgive her, too.

4. **Mourn and let "go" of your old relationship with your mother.** Your relationship with your mother will never be the same from this point on. Cry and let it all out!

5. **Find your inner mother.** She is your intuition. She is your mother wit. Activate her by using the pictures I asked you to gather from your younger self.

6. **Live your ideal life and re-establish relationship with your mother.** Establish new boundaries with your mother. Don't be harsh but be assertive and consistent when expressing them.

Note: It is important to do these steps even if your mother has passed away. Include a letter to her of everything you wished to tell her now, and if you had a good relationship with your mother, include a letter of gratitude.

Free Yourself from Father Drama

Now that we got mama out of the way, it is time to laser focus in on your daddy!

Our dads are such an important part of our lives because they share our first views of manhood and masculinity. The way in which your father did or did not present manhood to you matters because it helped not only shape your views on men but also on womanhood and femininity, including how it relates to masculinity.

We often times find ourselves in relationships that reflect or deflect from our relationships with our fathers as well. As divorce rates continue to plague our society and the number of single parent households continue to rise, more and more girls are growing up "fatherless" or receiving less than they should from the men in their lives.

Whether you barely knew your father or grew up with him in the same household, it is time you reflected on your relationship with these questions…

1. My father….. (or The absence of my father…..)

2. The fathering (or non-fathering) I received as a child was…..because….

3. The relationship my father and I have now is……

4. The things I love most about my father are…….

5. The things I dislike most about my father are…..

As mature women, we must learn to reflect on the past in ways that are constructive for our own personal growth and development. Reflecting on your relationship with your father should help you put into a clearer perspective the impact your father has on you both positively and/or negatively.

In order to begin healing this wound, there are a few key steps you must take:

1. **Admit the truth about your relationship.** Write down your truth: "I have a great relationship with my dad!!" "My father abandoned me at 5, and it still hurts like hell." "I had a distant father, and I act like I don't care. However, it bothers me to no end." "My dad left at 12, and I feel abandoned and always fear the men in my life will leave me too." List the truth that is easier.

2. **Forgive yourself and forgive him.** This step is crucial for women who have had absent, deadbeat, distant, or abusive fathers. Next, write down or say aloud that you forgive yourself and him. For example, "I forgive myself for …… as a result of my father ……."

3. **Accept your father for who he is.** Find a picture of him or visualize him being in front of you, and speak to him. Tell him that you forgive him and accept him for who he is and the choices he made.

4. **Let go of your old relationship with your father.** Release your old relationship with your father. The 4 year old, 12 years old, or 19 year old you may still be yearning for a certain type of relationship with your father. Focus on the here and now.

5. **Embrace a new relationship with your father.** Remind yourself that you can never gain back whatever may have been lost in the past with your father and your relationship with him. Make a list of things you are grateful for about your father, whether he was amazing or not.

Healing Your Childhood Drama Once and for All

Once you have completed both steps for both parents, it is time that you now really looked at the TRUTH from your parent's perspective. Every exercise up until this point has been about you.

However, healing is as much about you as it is about coming to peace, understanding, and acceptance of others.

Complete the following for each parent, and then say it aloud.

- TARIA PRITCHETT -

MOTHER

Although my mother _____
_____, my mother's truth is that she_____
_____.
However, I can choose to forgive her, accept her truth as different from my own, and love her no matter what. What my mother most needs and wants from me now is

_____
_____.

Though I cannot change her or her desires, I can change how I interact with her which from now on I will

_____
_____.

This way I still honor my mother yet still honor my own values and vision for my own life.

FATHER

Although my father _____
_____, my father's truth is that he_____
_____
_____.
However, I can choose to forgive him, accept his truth as different from my own, and love him no matter what. What my father most needs and wants from me now is_____

_____
_____.
Though I cannot change him or his desires, I can change how I interact with him which from now on I will
_____
_____.
This way I still honor my father yet still honor my own values and vision for my own life.

The greatest lesson you can learn from all past experiences whether it be with your parents, another family member, an ex, an old teacher, or a friend is that no one is to blame. We are here to become our most true and authentic selves. Inside the soul of every woman, is a strong desire to be her most confident and fierce self. All are called to fulfil that soul mission, but only some accept it.

Some women refuse to do the "inner work" it truly takes to become their best and live their best lives. There is no quick fix. This journey is real. It is deep. It can get messy and leave you teary eyed. It can also leave you confused and feeling like, "damn will I ever make it through." The truth is you will.

The fact that you are reading this book indicates to your own soul that you are READY! You can do this. You can truly become the woman you have always dreamed of being. This journey is again about you unbecoming everything you thought you were and becoming who you were really meant to be.

So every person, event, mistake, and experience is here to TEACH you how to become the woman you desire to be. Embrace the lessons. Learn from them. Grow from them. Evolve from them. Let go of everything that no longer serves you and where your life is now headed.

Always remember that all of it is necessary for you to walk the FIERCE path of true self-fulfilment and personal power. The process of healing the past is as much about reflection, forgiveness, and acceptance as it is about evolving you as a woman to a place where you are able to manifest and attract amazing things into your life that are no longer being blocked.

Note: Step-parents and guardians can also be included in the exercises provided in this chapter.

SELFIE CHECK

- What impact has my parents (or even my family) had on me as a grown woman?
- What parts of the healing processes mentioned will I try?
- What is the hardest part about forgiveness for me?

_____

The journey of true empowerment is not easy, but it is necessary. The journey to true self-love requires me to let go of the things that no longer serve me. For as I let them go, I become more of who I was destined to be.

#bornfierce

_____

Download your FREE workbook to complete
the selfie checks and exercises at:
www.unleashyourfierce.com/fierceworkbook

Chapter 5

RELEASE YOUR BAGGAGE

"Someone was hurt before you, wronged before you, hungry before you, frightened before you, beaten before you, humiliated before you, raped before you…yet, someone survived…You can do anything you choose to do."
– Maya Angelou

As you begin the journey of healing, evolving, and eventually becoming FIERCE, there is an order in which these items must occur in order for you to fully unleash the confident and fierce woman within yourself. Your parents and childhood are at the core of your being because they created you.

We don't get to choose our parents, but we do get to choose how we react to them. We do get to choose whether we will hold on to pain, failure, doubt, worry, fear, brokenness, blame, resentment, bitterness, and anger. You get to decide because you are in control of your own life.

It is imperative that you let all of those negative emotions and ways of being go. You must clear it away before you can begin the process of evolving into the woman you desire to be. Your past is a part of your story, but it doesn't have to define who you are today.

As Maya Angelou once said, "There is no greater agony than carrying an untold story inside of you." Did you know that Maya was sexually abused as a young girl at 8 years old?

Shortly after, she told her family members what had happened to her, and the next day she learned that the man who had violated her, which was her mother's boyfriend, was found dead. For a few years following this incident, she went mute. She didn't talk for five years. Maya Angelou, in all of her wisdom and poetic glory, did not talk.

This was the point in her life when she realized how powerful "words" could truly be. She thought her words had killed the man! She eventually started speaking again to her brother Bailey, and girl am I glad she did because she has given us some of the most profound phrases, quotes, and insights through her own words!

The point is that Maya learned a few valuable lessons, and one is that what we speak and let out are powerful. They can have a negative or positive effect. Either way, they remove the burden of suffering in silence.

Believe it or not, when you walk around holding pain and the past in, it shows! It is reflected in your aura, and others can tell even if you don't say a word. It is your responsibility to set yourself FREE. We are all fighting our own battles, and if we're not careful, we will overlook our own mess in favor of thinking someone else has it worse than us.

- TARIA PRITCHETT -

We are all given personal challenges to overcome. You know what yours are. Acknowledge Them. Deal with Them. Heal Them. Evolve to the next stage in your own life as a happy, healthy, healed, and whole woman.

A woman can never be complete if she is broken and her past has yet to be healed.

Whatever you do, release the broken and unresolved parts of yourself.

Some of the best ways to do this is to:

☐ Get counselling from a trusted and certified heath care professional and work through specific issues.

☐ Get a cute journal and write out your feelings and thoughts. Get a canvas and paint your sorrow. Get some paper and pen a song. Get in some yoga pants and stretch your pain away. Whatever brings you joy and happiness, use that medium to release your past.

☐ Volunteer to work with youth or younger girls (or reconnect more closely with your daughter or nieces/younger cousins) by giving to someone else what you would hope to gain. In turn, you will start healing yourself. Children have a way of making you want to become your best self in order to present your own self and life as the best.

☐ Get coaching by an empowerment or life coach like myself, who can help you pinpoint your wounds and blocks and help you heal them so that you can evolve as a woman.

☐ Allow a kinesiologist or energy healer to help you locate the blockages in your body and being. Research a good one in your area.

☐ Listen to an intuitive healer or spiritual strategist to discover what might be blocking you at a soul and spiritual level, and/or get a tarot or astrology reading that draws on parts of yourself you never really considered regarding your personality and life path.

Select whichever ones feel right to you, but also don't limit what you can do by staying in your comfort zone. The consequence for refusing this process is that what you resist, will persist. You can keep trying to move forward, but any underlying baggage will block your forward motion.

For example:

Your Desire: Marry a smart, sexy, and successful high quality man who treats you like a queen.

Your Baggage: Father was emotionally and physically absent most of your life, and now you're uncomfortable building trust in men.

Your Underlying Belief: Don't think you are worthy of having that kind of man and repeatedly end up with men who cheat, and prove themselves to be untrustworthy.

Your Desire: Earn $20,000 more in income to cover additional expenses and excursions and stop using credit cards

Your Baggage: Growing up your mother was very cheap, and constantly struggled to pay bills.

Your Underlying Belief: Money is scarce, and it is not enough money for you to be happy at any given time. Cling to credit cards because they give the illusion that you have more money to spend.

Your Desire: Lose weight and drop 3 dress sizes

Your Baggage: Constantly worried about what other people will think because you were bullied in school, and by your siblings for being chubbier and being smarter than others.

Your Underlying Belief: You must hide yourself from others, and your fat is your security blanket.

Identify what I like to call your core "confidence barriers". This is the baggage that weighs you down that you usually don't consider. It is hard to have a strong belief in yourself and your abilities when there is something that could always stop your progress.

Unless....you deal with it and heal it! Once you begin the healing process, two of the main questions you will have is how long will this take, and how will I know it is healed.

The truth is healing can take anywhere from 2 weeks to 2 months to 2 years. This is a journey. You are on a path. This is a season, and they don't last forever. Once the season begins, you must give yourself time to go through this process. You are going to fail, stumble, fall back into your old ways, forgive yourself, fall again, get back up, make progress, feel stuck, and feel change....the road to healing does not have a specific time frame.

Choosing to embrace this season means also choosing to allow everything to happen in divine order and time, which means you must surrender to the experience at hand.

Allow your soul to guide you. Allow your intuition to lead you through because it will strengthen you during this time if you follow through with this. You will begin to feel it, and you will begin to have a knowing of how far you have come and how much left you have to go. You'll know you are healed when the same situation, person, or experience is presented to you and you feel, think, and act a different way on the inside.

One of the most timeless and most powerful ways to release the "old" and embrace the "new" is to literally immerse yourself in a "Healing Bath." Healing baths are the perfect way to release negative energy, toxins, and baggage both physically and spiritually.

HEALING BATH

Please set aside some quality "me time" to complete this exercise. Baths are spiritual and detoxifying rituals that have been around for centuries because of their healing nature. All women deserve healing, pleasure, and pampering. You are no different sweetie!

Enjoy!

You will need:

- Bubble bath with Epsom Salt
- Rose Oil
- Lavender Oil
- 1-2 Cups of Milk (optional)
- ½ Cup of Honey (optional)
- Light Pink, White or Light Blue Candles (optional)
- Small Pillow (optional to rest head)
- Washcloth
- Rose Petals
- Healing Affirmations (Write on cards or a sheet of paper such as "I am happy, healthy, healed, and whole. I forgive my mother and father and set myself free to accept them as they are. Although my father left me, I still deeply love and accept myself.

Even though I have made many mistakes in my relationships, I forgive myself and still love myself no matter what")

You will:

1. Gather all materials prior to starting this exercise and clean bathroom thoroughly.

2. Allow the bath water to run and just before you get in, add in the oil to preserve its natural properties. Add in Epsom salt, milk, honey, and rose petals as bath is running, and light candles.

3. Enter bath and sit quietly for the first 5 minutes with your eyes closed. Try your best to clear your mind and meditate.

4. Say your healing affirmations aloud.

5. Close your eyes, and using a washcloth, gently wash away all things that no longer serve you. Voice it!

For example:

"God please release all of my doubts, fears, worries, baggage, unresolved issues, resentments, toxic ties and heal me. Make me whole. Make me complete. Make me into the woman I desire, deserve, and was destined to be. Make me into the woman that you divinely designed me to be, restore me to a being of love, allow me to radiate light, and allow me to unleash the confident and fierce woman within. Thank you Lord. It's done. Show me."

6. Keep your eyes closed and quiet your mind. Listen to the voice within. Allow your intuition to guide you. Listen for God's voice and allow him to speak to you. Ask him questions if you desire. Listen for his words and wisdom.

7. Conclude your bath by drying off and putting on something that makes you feel restored and beautiful. Then reflect on this experience through a medium that is best for you whether it be through writing, song, art, etc. Just be sure to document it some way because you want to be able to reflect on your entire journey, especially once you make it through your healing season. I highly recommend writing it if you can.

**Do a "healing bath" as often as possible to restore and refresh yourself. As you grow and change, update your affirmations to fit the state you are currently in, and create specific prayers to reflect the specific things you need to deal with and heal.

Here is an example for more self-love and self-confidence:

"Dear God, Please remove any barriers that block me from loving myself and fully operating in my power as a woman. Take away my insecurities and remind me of my value. I surrender my fears to you, and I ask that you show me whom I am meant to be. God you are in me and I am in you. So I simply cannot fail. Empower me Lord so that I may love myself better, and I may walk and talk with the confidence you have placed in me. Amen"

Here is another example prayer for love:

"Dear God, Thank you for loving me. Please remove any walls that are in front of my heart. Help me heal any parts of myself that are blocking me from the love I divinely deserve and desire. Please show me how to keep loving myself like you love me and how to open my heart to love others. Help me become the best woman I can be so I can attract the man you have designed just for me. Send me a man I can grow with, open my heart to, spiritually align with, and someone whom I can manifest your vision for us together with. Show me how to prepare for this. Amen."

Here is another example prayer for life:

"Dear God, You are always guiding and directing my footsteps. I recognize that everything is working together. I have faith in you and I have faith in my journey. Lord show me how to be fearless and faithful at all times. For you know the plans you have for me. Plans to prosper me and bless me. I free myself from suffering, and I surrender to divine flow. Despite any thoughts I have that may dim my light, Lord, please show me how to believe in my power and instead glow with love and light. I know that within you lies the answer to any question I have. Amen"

- TARIA PRITCHETT -

SELFIE CHECK

- What baggage is currently weighing me down?
- How would my life change if I were baggage free?
- What suggestion will I try to aid me on my healing journey?

I refuse to let my baggage block my power and my blessings. I free up space in my heart, mind, and soul to receive goodness. I am worthy of living an empowered, prosperous, and fulfilling life.

#bornfierce

Download your FREE workbook to complete the selfie checks and get a healing bath printable at:
www.unleashyourfierce.com/fierceworkbook

– PART III –

∞

FALL IN LOVE WITH YOURSELF

Chapter 6

BECOME CONFIDENT & EMPOWERED

"Our deepest fear is not that we are inadequate. Our deepest fear is that we are powerful beyond measure. It is our light, not our darkness that most frightens us. We ask ourselves, 'Who am I to be brilliant, gorgeous, talented, fabulous?' Actually, who are you not to be?"
- Marianne Williamson

Once a woman has healed parts of herself that block her FIERCE radiance, she naturally moves into a state of authentic, fierce womanhood. It is the state that all women secretly desire to achieve at some point in their lives. A confident and fierce woman is: A woman who accepts herself (with flaws and all), embraces her culture and power as a highly valuable and magnetic woman, and lives a highly fulfilling, satisfying, happy, and successful life.

We all know a **bold, confident, and FIERCE woman** when we meet her. She is show stopping, and she turns heads in any room. Men fall for her effortlessly. Women envy her zest for life and try to compete or even imitate. She appears to have it all. She has beauty, style, brilliance, purpose, success, a great man, exciting life, and last but certainly not least, a glow like no other.

She radiates. She is regal. She has embraced her real self from the core. She is regal realness. It is easier said than done to become this type of woman.

The quote at the beginning of this chapter states that our biggest fear is that we are "inadequate." As women, we often feel we are not enough, not valuable enough, not worthy enough, not confident enough, not good enough, not thin enough, not beautiful enough, and so on. This leads us to dull our shine because we refuse to fully love ourselves unconditionally.

Often times we turn to men, material things, money, and the media to fill this void. We are starving for love, affection, and attention from all the wrong places because we refuse to go through the process of healing those parts of ourselves that block our natural confidence and radiance.

As we move past our childhood wounds, we can start to unravel the next layer of underlying beliefs that hold us back from being the confident and fierce women we desire to be. As women, we all desire to fully step into our power, live out our fullest potential, be confident in ourselves, love, accept, and forgive ourselves, and live a good life.

However, it is scary to step into your power. We fear rejection. We fear shame. We fear abandonment. We fear judgement. We fear our own power.

My questions for you: What would you do if you knew you couldn't fail? Where are you holding yourself back from being great? Are you giving yourself permission to be great or waiting for others to give you validation?

As we get closer to becoming our most empowered selves, we begin to hit walls which often lead to procrastination, sabotage, and fear. Becoming more fierce forces you to make a decision which is either to stretch or to shrink. Either stretch yourself to go to the next level or shrink back to safety in your comfort zone. Will you stretch or will you shrink?

Stretching is hard and shrinking is hard. Choose your hard. You ever stepped outside your comfort zone, stretched yourself, took a risk, stepped out on faith and tried something new, but inside you feel some kind of way, either you physically feel sick, start to worry, or even criticize yourself or others? If so, then you are human! What has happened is that you have hit your "upper limit."

Recently, I read *The Big Leap* by Gay Hendricks. Hendricks argues that all of us should be living from what he calls our "Zone of Genius." This is our most confident and empowered self, living our best life and fulfilling our God given purpose. The place we all desire to be.

However, so many of us never make it there because our 'zone of genius' is above the "limit of success" we think we can have. Once we move beyond our usual habits, thoughts, and actions and start moving closer to our zone of genius, we tend to sabotage ourselves so that we shrink back into the familiar zone of living we are used to.

There are 4 major barriers, according to Hendricks that keep us "limited" and unable to fully own our confidence and live the life we desire and deserve.

Read through the 4 and identify which 1 or 2 are currently holding you back:

1. Believing You Are Flawed

Think you are bad or unworthy in some way and don't deserve good things to happen to you. If good happens, you find a way to sabotage it. As a result, you play it safe and stay small.

2. Believing That By Becoming More Confident & Living A Better Life You Will Be Disloyal And/Or Leave People Behind In The Past

Think we are being disloyal to our roots/family/friends if we rise above where they are and in turn, might potentially become abandoned or rejected

3. Believe That You Are A Burden In The World

Think you must sabotage success so you won't be a bigger burden, especially if you are still carrying childhood baggage with you

4. Believe That You Must Dim Your Light So That You Won't Outshine Someone Else

Think you must hold back fully expressing who you really are so you don't look, do, feel, and live better than others, especially true for smart and successful women!

Regardless of how much progress you make on your self-love and confidence journey and no matter how successful you become, your "barriers" will continue to pop up every time you try to make a new "LEAP" in your life. It is a brave and courageous act to personally develop yourself. Some days are easy. Some days are hard. But, it beats being unhappy and unfulfilled any day.

Women who have stretched themselves to become confident and fierce all have the same characteristics which are as follows:

1. She knows her worth.

She recognizes that she is regal, beautiful, and divine. A woman who is worthy of all good things to come into her life: good life, good men, good body image, good clothing and shoes, good food, good jobs/career, and good blessings. Ultimately, she believes she is worthy of winning at any area in her life

2. She loves herself.

She loves herself unconditionally. She knows who she is because she believes in a power higher than herself. She knows she has purpose. She knows she is special. She knows she deserves to live well and be treated well. She takes pride in honoring herself, making time for herself, fulfilling her calling, and doing things that feed her soul and make her happy.

3. She accepts herself flaws and all.

She has accepted her real and authentic self. She knows she is not perfect. She knows she is flawed yet still beautiful and worthy.

She knows that her failures, setbacks, mistakes, and past hurts do not define her. She grows through whatever it is that she is going through in her life. Yet, she embraces them, forgives them, and heals herself from them.

4. She looks in the mirror and smiles.

When she looks in the mirror, she sees beauty. She sees the most beautiful girl in the world. She thinks positive and speaks nothing but love to herself. Whether she is a size 2, 12, or 20, she loves what she is at any given moment.

5. She sees other women as collaborators rather than competition.

She recognizes that there will always be someone better than her, but no one will ever be her. This is her power. Therefore, she rather compliment than compete, and instead collaborate to make a greater contribution to society. She inspires others to want better. By the way she lives her life, her life sends a message. It makes other women want to become better and become their best. She is inspiring, motivating, and uplifting.

7. Her presence is obvious and noticed.

People recognize her when she speaks or enters a room. Her energy is positive and fierce. A man can recognize her magnetism without even talking to her because he can feel her energy and see her FIERCE glow. This attracts him because he knows he will have to work harder to get a woman who knows who she is and what she wants out of life. She is magnetic and one-of-a kind.

8. She attracts high quality men (or man).

She attracts men at a higher caliber who love her, honor her, cherish her, and value her. She is marriage material, whether she wants to marry or not. But her vibe attracts men of quality who treat her like a Queen and act like REAL men because she treats herself that way already.

9. She takes pride in her appearance.

She walks out of the house fierce and fly. She rocks her own unique style and owns it! She never looks run down, sloppy, or dishevelled. It is evident she puts thought into what she was going to wear, and put effort into doing her hair for the day. She dresses for her body type and pairs it with her own style, depending on the time and place, often times making a fashion statement in her own unique way.

10. She is living her dream life.

She is either working towards or living out the life she has always dreamed of. She may help others build their dreams, but she also invests quality time and money into her own dream, hustle, or desired lifestyle.

It may be hard to believe, but there are women in the world who operate from this place every day. At first glance, this type of women may seem "perfect" and often women will compare themselves to a woman of such caliber.

However, no human being is perfect. Not one single person. No one feels 100% happy all of the time or even feels confident all of the time. No one always wins 100% of the time every single day. It's normal. Everybody has a bad day or a rough season. No one is exempt from failure, rejection, shame, setbacks, or fear.

You are allowed to feel like shit! Just don't make it a habit. What makes the confident woman different is that she knows all of that, and she keeps going. She doesn't give up. She may stop to cry, scream, pray, journal, or vent to a friend, but home girl is going to persevere. She will dust her cute self off and try again.

It will always be someone or something to suggest that you aren't good enough. Someone will always tell you "no." Sometimes you will make mistakes. Sometimes fear and doubt will shut down any courage and confidence you have. Your job is to keep going. Keep it moving.

As you move, your confidence increases a notch each time. When it is a setback, it has set you up to go to the next level of confidence because as my mom always taught me, "what don't kill you only makes you stronger." So, you are way stronger and more confident than you think girlfriend! Own it!

Here's why:

Millionaire & TV Mogul, Oprah Winfrey, in an interview with the Baltimore Sun reflects on being fired from her news anchor position when she worked in Baltimore because she "wasn't fit for television", and even shamed for her name. Her co-host would frequently say "what is an Oprah?" *Yet, she kept going even with the pain and rejection she must have felt. She went from "unfit" to being unstoppable and owning her own television network, becoming a billionaire, and having one of the highest ranked television shows of all time.*

Grammy Award-winning Singer & Songwriter, Alicia Keys in a blog titled, *A Revelation*, posted on her website explains why she used to dress as a tomboy when she started her singing career. She admits she did it to stave off attention from men. The clothes allowed her to hide her true beauty as a woman.

However, she soon realized that she was misjudged as being "gay" and "hard" which she wasn't. So she started dressing more feminine. She declares, "And just the other day it hit me! OMG! Alicia!!! Why are you choosing to be that person?? That is so old and outdated!! STOP!!....I don't have to hide anymore. I don't have to pretend and hold back. I don't have to think that my intelligence, beauty and sensuality are intimidating to others. [...] I don't have to think my silliness, clumsiness, or hallmark card optimism, is something I can't be proud of!"

She kept going. She wasn't perfect, but she found her true self by learning to love herself and honor who she really was even though it took trial and error. She eventually had her breakthrough and increased her confidence.

Actress Gabrielle Union revealed in her 2013 Essence Magazine Hollywood Luncheon that she has struggled with self-esteem issues. She admitted to pretending to be something she wasn't, shrinking when other "dope women" were in her presence, and spreading gossip and rumors about her fellow actresses when she felt like they outshined her.

She told the audience, "It's easy to pretend to be "fierce and fearless" because living your truth takes real courage. Real fearless and fierce women admit mistakes and they work to correct them."

She kept going. She learned from her mistakes. She forgave herself. She took the time to let go of limiting beliefs that did not serve her or others. As a result, she increased her confidence and changed her mind set for the better.

The common theme: You have to commit to yourself always. No one else may believe in you. Other things may get in your way. People may talk about you. Opportunities may reject you. You may fail over and over again. Your past may not be pretty. Limiting beliefs may pop up.

But you have to believe in yourself, you have to use life experiences as your teachers, and you have to recognize when you are holding yourself back from greatness and correct yourself so you can be more fierce.

- TARIA PRITCHETT -

SELFIE CHECK

- Which of the ten characteristics of confident women resonated with me?

- How am I holding myself back from my greatness?

- What can I take away from the celebrity examples shared?

---

*Confidence is my birthright.
I can either stretch into it or shrink back into my comfort zone. The choice is mine.*

#bornfierce

---

*Download your FREE workbook to complete
the selfie checks at: www.unleashyourfierce.com/fierceworkbook*

Chapter 7

STEP-UP YOUR
SELF-LOVE & SELF-WORTH

"I'm the first example of how the world is supposed to love me, and I have to give them the best example ever."
-Lisa Nichols

When a woman chooses to stretch into her most confident and fierce self, she has to step up her daily routines, daily thoughts, and daily actions. When I decided to turn my women's empowerment blog into a business, I learned that being an entrepreneur is the best form of personal development in the world. It requires you to stretch yourself beyond your wildest dreams. It forced me to really own who I was, step into my power fully, and believe in myself more than ever!

I learned how to fully commit to myself and my dreams like never before. As I began to learn the beauty of building a brand and motivating women worldwide I discovered that there were a ton of ways I needed to step up in every area of my own life.

I failed multiple times, I fell short on having extra income to build my dream life and business, I made no sales even after launching a new product, I was inconsistent with connecting with my clients and customers, and I treated my business as a hobby. If you can imagine, doubt, fear, worry, and unworthiness settled in from time to time as a result. It didn't feel good.

I had a clear vision for my life and business, and I was working hard to make it happen, so I thought, and I was frustrated because what I envisioned wasn't coming into fruition. I knew I had a message that I needed to get to the masses so instead of having a pity party, I sought help to empower me to take a leap to the next level of my life. I was sick and tired of not being my most confident and empowered self and living the life I knew I desired and deserved.

This all changed when I began to see how valuable my contribution to the world really was. Ultimately, I had to change the story I was telling myself. I had to get out of a mindset that believed I wasn't good enough to do xyz or wasn't experienced enough to do xyz or wasn't skilled enough to do xyz. By shifting my thoughts, I was able to take action and start to see my confidence grow and my business progress.

Inspirational speaker, writer, and creator of *The Desire Map*, Danielle Laporte, did an experiment that showed the effects our mind and thoughts have on our sense of self. Along with her son, Danielle split an apple in half and placed a half in two separate containers.

For about 25 days they spoke positive words over one apple such as "you're awesome" and negative words to the other such as "You're not worthy of my attention because you're gonna rot."

Lo and behold, by the end of the 25 days or so, they checked both apple pieces.

One of them rotted, while the other one still looked perfectly fine. This shows that your words have meaning, and what you feed yourself matters—literally and figuratively. We are the ones who can speak life into ourselves, but there is only one way to wake up to this fact.

The secret to becoming the confident and fierce woman you desire to be is to AWAKEN!

To be awakened is the process of becoming aware of something. To become aware is to shift. Shifting is the process of becoming. Becoming is a feminine process of healing, evolving, and growing into the woman you desire to be. A woman will never ever feel like she is enough unless she shifts her mindset and changes her thoughts.

In a recent interview, Oprah Winfrey said, "I live a fantastic life. My inner life is really intact. I live from the inside out. Everything that I have, I have because I let it be fueled by who I am....I work at staying awake."

Your level of negative self-talk, the level of money you are currently making, your current occupation, your current relationship status, and so on are all in direct proportion to how awake you are on the inside.

Your inner life is reflected on the outside in every area of your life. Your feelings of un-fulfillment are reflected in that 20 pound weight gain. Your belief that you are unworthy is reflected in the men who currently are and have cheated on you. Your thoughts of life being so hard are reflected in your day to day struggles. Your poverty mindset is reflected through your current bank account number. Your fear that you aren't good enough is reflected in you not being offered that job opportunity. Your constant doubting is reflected in you not currently working at your dream job.

You will never feel any level of progression into the next level in your life until you are willing to do what Oprah calls the "consciousness work". It requires for you to wholeheartedly love yourself, believe in yourself, and become the best you can be.

In order for you to fall madly in love with yourself, which by the way can be done even if you haven't for years, you must commit to yourself at the deepest level.

HERE ARE 10 WAYS TO COMMIT TO YOURSELF

Know your worth

This is a mindset shift. You must learn to validate yourself by deciding who you will be and declaring that. No one can take away your belief. Haters, doubters, and naysayers will always be around and so will failure, defeat, and mistakes. They don't qualify you, God does. Allow God to rise up within you. If He is in you, girlfriend, you cannot fail.

Silence Your Inner Critic

Quiet the negative voices in your heard that try to derail you from moving forward. The more you criticize yourself, the more license others feel to criticize you. Criticism that is not constructive operates at a very low vibration, and the energy is not positive. You don't want to give that vibe off to others. Affirmations are especially good for silencing this critic.

Let Failure Fuel You

Failure is inevitable. Failure is one of life's greatest teachers. Use it to make you stronger. Use it to fuel your hunger to become better. Use it as a stepping stone to greatness. Use it as fuel to succeed and overcome even more.

Always remember:

☐ Before Scandal, Kerry Washington piloted the lead role for two other shows which got picked up; however, she was replaced because she wasn't "black enough". Scandal came shortly after and has become one of the most highly rated and watched shows in American television history.

☐ Author of the Harry Pottery series, JK Rowling wrote her famous book series while unemployed, recently divorced, and a single mother in a café. Her early writings were on dinner napkins. She was rejected by 12 publishers; however, her books have went on to become the best- selling book series in history, become a movie series, and even have a theme park called, The Wizarding World of Harry Potter, in Walt Disney World.

☐ Marilyn Monroe was told she was not beautiful enough for film and was told she should become a secretary. Say what you want, but for her to not be "beautiful", she has went on to become a beauty and cultural icon with millions of people rocking t-shirts, posting pictures, and putting up posters with her face on it.

Listen to Your Intuition

Get quiet. Get alone. Spend time with just yourself. Make self-trust a priority. Take a personal day from work. Meditate in the morning when you wake up. Pray before you leave the house every day. Sit in silence more often. Solitude is where you will find solutions, strength, and strategies to implement in your life. Learn to slow down more, and use journaling to own your voice and truly hear your inner wisdom speak to you. Your intuition will never stir you wrong.

Follow Your Boundaries

Even if you have to literally write them down, do it. You teach people how to treat you, but you also have to be clear on what that means. Also, people only treat you how you treat yourself. Identify what mental, emotional, physical, spiritual, professional, and relational limits will be in your life.

Follow them. Ensure that others do also by telling someone "no" or saying how you feel. Each time you stand up for yourself, your confidence will grow.

Feed Your Soul

Invest time and money into feeding yourself with motivational, inspirational, and uplifting material. Whether it is audios, CD's, books, workbooks, magazines, seminars, online courses, positive social media pages, home study programs, and so on, fill your life with positivity. Fill your soul with empowering content at all times. It will help you shift your mindset and help you elevate how you feel about yourself. Allocate a portion of your income to both your personal and professional growth for best results.

Surround Yourself with Like Minded People

You become like the five people you hang around the most. Choose wisely. Connect and collaborate with like-minded individuals. Even find and spend time with women who are more confident and empowered than you. See how they live their lives, how they dress, how they talk, how they interact with people, and so on. This will cut your own learning curve and allow you to become the woman you desire to be quicker. If finding like-minded people is a struggle, join Facebook groups, start a Meetup.com account, or attend conferences and seminars to find women who are on your level.

Stop Comparing Yourself

So often we get into the need of comparing ourselves to others! I call it OCD: Obsessive Comparison Disorder!

Shay already brought a house, and I still live here. Tamika is already married with kids at 28, and I can't find a man. Lena already moved out, yet I'm still living at home. Monique already started a business so now I can't because she already has it going on. Renee has "good hair" and a cute face so I couldn't possibly love my 4c hair and this dark skin of mine. Jasmine's has such a great husband, yet I'm going through a divorce. I'll never find a love like that. Emily lost all that weight, but she had a trainer, and I can't afford that...and so on!!

Blah Blah! Again, more excuses that force you to shrink back into your comfort zone. Stop it right now!

Reflect on this comparison wisdom from business and brand coach Amanda Miller Littlejohn: *"But what if Lorraine Hansberry refused to write plays because Gwendolyn Brooks was penning poems and Zora Neale Hurston was killing it with her fiction? What if Toni Morrison and Maya Angelou decided to never pick up a pen because their literary godmothers had already done it so well? They all belong to the same canon of African-American literature. Yet, somehow there was room for all of their voices, and the world is still hungry for more."*

Simply, be your own kind of beautiful. You are already qualified. You have already been called to greatness. Don't dim your light because you think others are already shining. We can never have too much light in the world.

Revamp Your Environment

Declutter your home, car, purse, and work space. Clutter clouds confidence, and it blocks blessings. Once you declutter, set your space up for confident and empowered living. Select themes for your space, add in new colors, paint your walls, add in new scents, and accentuate with confidence reminders such as motivational sayings on canvases, inspirational magnets, and vision boards on the walls.

Validate Yourself

Give yourself permission to be great. Stop waiting for other people to tell you what to do. Stop worrying about what other people think. Stop wishing, wondering, and waiting when it will be a good time to make your next move. Move now. On your own time. In your own way. As Nike says, "Just Do It."

Give yourself a "go" on becoming confident, bold, and fearless. Not only must you commit to yourself, you must also get real with yourself. Determine where you currently stand in your life… A confident and fierce woman is a self-loving woman.

Self-love is the all-encompassing, unconditional state of caring deeply and honoring one-self completely. Self-love encompasses a number of areas that a woman must evolve within herself.

Consider my Twelve Tenets of Self-Love. Each tenet reflects an aspect of self-love. Self-love is an umbrella and underneath it houses all of the different layers that contribute to it for an individual.

Read each one. Reflect on it. Rate yourself. Using the chart that follows: Where are you thriving, and where are you falling short on a scale from 1-10, 1 being needs serious improvement to 10 being doing well.

Self-Care- How much time and attention do you give yourself? How much care do you provide yourself beyond being pampered at the nail salon or getting your hair done?

Self-Awareness- How awake are you to what is really going on inside of you and your life? How well do you really know yourself?

Self-Acceptance- How much do you accept yourself as you are? Do you ever deflect your beauty or brilliance?

Self-Trust- How much do you trust yourself? How much do you follow your intuition and make sound decisions?

Self-Esteem- How worthy do you feel on the inside? Do you believe in yourself and your abilities?

Self-Compassion- How kind are you to yourself? Do you talk to yourself like you love yourself? Do you forgive yourself easily?

Self-Empowerment- How much control do you feel you have over your life? How happy are you with yourself and your life? Are you achieving your goals?

Self-Expression- How well do you express yourself to others? How well do you express who you really are? Do you own your voice?

Self-Pleasure- How much joy, bliss, happiness, and fun is present in your life?

Self-Discipline- Do you follow through? Are you meeting deadlines and achieving goals? Are you managing your time and life well? Are you stressed and overwhelmed often?

Self-Respect- Do you honor, cherish, and value yourself? Do you expect others to? Do others take advantage of you?

Self-Forgiveness- Do you blame yourself? Do you beat yourself up for things that you need to let go of?

Tenet	Your Rating	Explanation of Rating
1. Self-Care	....	....
2. Self-Awareness	....	....
3. Self-Acceptance	....	....
4. Self-Trust	....	....
5. Self-Esteem	....	....
6. Self-Compassion	....	....
7. Self-Empowerment	....	....
8. Self-Expression	....	....
9. Self-Pleasure	....	....
10. Self-Discipline	....	....
11. Self-Respect	....	....
12. Self-Forgiveness	....	....

It is no easy feat to feel complete balance in every single one of these areas. However, in order to increase your self-love, you must create a plan to grow in the areas where you scored lower and to reinforce the areas that you are already doing well in.

Here are simple power moves you can take depending on where you need to evolve:

Self-Care	Devote one day per week to yourself, and schedule a self-love play date.
Self-Awareness	Get to know yourself by taking a personality quiz. Can be found online.
Self-Acceptance	Create a mantra and repeat daily until you begin to believe it.

Self-Trust	Pray more. Tap into your feelings. Follow your intuition more.
Self-Esteem	Feed yourself at the soul and spiritual levels (i.e. books, audio, video, etc.)
Self-Compassion	Find your inner mother and talk to yourself like you love yourself.
Self-Empowerment	Take more control of your life by setting goals, and taking daily actions to achieve them.
Self-Expression	Express yourself more in settings where you usually don't.
Self-Pleasure	Do more of what brings you happiness, bliss, and joy.
Self-Discipline	Create a daily routine and stick to it.
Self-Respect	Set boundaries with others and follow them.
Self-Forgiveness	Write yourself a forgiveness letter.

These are just a few small steps you can start taking today. There are a host of others for each tenet. Utilize the chart as a jumpstart on your confidence journey.

Empowerment starts with "self." Being fierce means you have an evolved self. The word *evolve* includes the word "love" backwards: evolve, which means that your empowerment is rooted in your self-love practices. A fierce woman is free to simply be herself, but she doesn't sit around waiting for it to happen. She makes it happen on her own!

Ensure you are regularly using the tenets in this chapter to measure where you are with your self-love.

SELFIE CHECK:

- What does being more self-loving mean to me?
- How will I start committing to myself more?
- Which tenets of self-love do I need to work on more?

Self-love is a commitment I make to myself.
By committing to myself, I honor myself.
When I honor myself, I love myself.
When I love myself, my confidence strengthens.
When my confidence strengthens, I am empowered to succeed.

#bornfierce

Download your FREE workbook to complete the selfie checks and exercises at: www.unleashyourfierce.com/fierceworkbook

Chapter 8

COMMIT TO CONFIDENCE DAILY

"You are you own best thing."
— *Toni Morrison*

If self-love is the business of doing all of the inner work, then confidence is the business of showing the outside world all of the hard work you've been doing. If you want to be a "girl on fire" all the time, then you better make sure you are giving yourself that love daily.

You get up in the morning and brush your teeth every day, kiss your man every day, get your cup of coffee every morning, or wrap your hair every night. Just like you do those things you do every day, you have got to commit to building in confidence boosters daily.

One of the biggest issues I hear when I talk to clients is that they don't commit to maintaining their confidence on a daily basis. They are aware that they should, but they usually leave this out because they are "so busy" living their lives that they don't have the time to commit to themselves. However, boosting and then maintaining your confidence should be included in your day to day routine for maximum results. If you can't include at least just 5 minutes of self-loving on your daily agenda, how can you ever expect to fully unleash the confident and fierce woman within yourself?

You are your own best thing. If you don't cater to yourself, then who will? The best way to unleash the confident woman within yourself is to affirm yourself and "act as if" you already are!

A recent study showed that the brain waves generated and neurotransmitters released when someone, for example, visualizes flying on a plane are exactly the same as the brain waves of a person who is actually on a plane.

Your mind and the Universe doesn't recognize the difference between what you perceive as "real" and "imaginary." It only reads vibration. The easiest way to attract something is to evoke the feeling and vibration of already having it present in your life. Your energy and vibration are very important factors when it comes to falling in love with yourself and being FIERCE everywhere you go.

The most confident, fierce, and successful women in the world already know this. Upon waking up and going to sleep, they have a solid routine that helps them stay focused and committed to their well-being and living a healthy, wealthy, and beautiful life.

For example, upon waking, ditch checking social media or watching TV and wake up at least 30 minutes earlier than usual. During this time in which I call a "confidence routine", do the following: meditate or visualize some aspect of your life that you desire to happen that day or in the near future, pray or say daily devotion, review your vision boards, and say affirmations to start your day off consciously evoking feelings of confidence, happiness, love, success, and miracles to come your way.

This routine was inspired by world renowned life coach, Anthony Robbins who believes in "Hour of Power" to begin each day. He also believes that "success leaves clues", and he found that the most successful people in the world started their days off with a routine that over time created better habits and overall better quality of life.

Simply put, confident, fierce, and successful women do things differently and go the extra mile to constantly be in a state of FIERCE. Disciplining yourself to ensure you have a confidence routine in your life will change your whole life! It is a commitment.

Start by adding in one thing per day such as saying one short affirmation each morning, add in saying a prayer, and then add in reviewing your vision board. Another positive way to ensure you stay committed to this empowering daily ritual is to create an "empowerment zone" in your bedroom or home that will serve as your personal place of peace.

Call it what you want, your sacred space, prayer room, spiritual altar, self-love station, or confidence corner…but you need one. Adorn it with pictures, your favorite bible verses, poetry and song snippets, empowering art work, candles, quotations, journals, flowers, vision boards, gratitude jar, and anything else that is meaningful to you. Stop in this space once per day, light candles, and pray.

Go in this space when you need sacred time alone to refuel and recharge yourself. It is a space for you regain your energy too because as women, we give a lot to the world. Use this space to fill yourself back up. When you are filled, you can then overflow more into the world and others. If you live with others, you can discuss your boundaries with this space or purchase a colorful photo storage box to place your items in and take your sacred space with you to a more private place. You can use this space to jumpstart your morning, ignite your day, or power down your night.

In addition to establishing a daily routine, it is imperative that you also set up your life & style to reflect the confidence you are inspiring within yourself.

Here Are Some Additional Power Moves You Can Implement Immediately In Your Life For A Confidence Boost

Empower Your Showers

Turn your normal routine showers into an empowering sauna of self-love! Use shower time to not only clean your body, but to connect deeply with yourself. This will require a longer time in the shower, but it is worth it.

Start exfoliating daily when you shower. Include time to say a prayer to a higher power and to say several affirmations to yourself before you get your day started. Supercharge it by massaging your body with your favorite body wash and saying your affirmations at the same time.

Afterwards, lotion up gently and send love to each part of your body. Be present and embrace the water, your body, and your words. Do this every day and walk out feeling electrified to start your day! Take this a step further and take a bath at least once a week to really connect more deeply with yourself.

Carry Your Confidence

Make it your business to affirm your love for yourself daily. Do this by creating "confidence cards" that you carry with you. Each card should include visual images that activate your desired outcome and an affirmation statement that you say daily. Refer to the "Appendix of Affirmations" at the end of this book for ideas.

For example, "I am a regal and magnetic woman", "I am a man magnet, and all men want to date me", "I am a queen, and I am a high value woman who never settles for less than the best", "I am a happy, healthy, and whole woman, and I attract good things my way at all times", and the list continues.

Pull these cards out when you need them the most. Again, just like you brush your teeth every day, you need to also keep your mind fresh and anew by telling yourself sweet nothings daily, especially when you are worrying, doubting, or fearing something in your life.

Dress in Your Best

No matter where you are going always, ALWAYS dress your best. Your image determines your interactions. People will approach and address you based upon how you are dressed. People will perceive you based on what you put out there. If you want to be a FIERCE, confident, and magnetic woman, then you must dress like that woman!

A woman who attracts high quality opportunities, men, finances, and so on has to dress the part. Like attracts like. Every morning you should walk out the house flawless. I don't care if you are running to the dollar store. Look your absolute best! People address, judge, and make decisions about you based on not only your vibe on the inside, but the life you are (or are not) presenting on the outside.

Put it this way, you should look so good that you make other woman want to get their *ish* together! Look good EVERYWHERE! When you look good, you feel good, too. If this is an area you need to upgrade, create a style look book using images from magazines and inspiration you find online and through social media. Include every aspect: hair, nails, shoes, accessories, clothes, and so on. Throw out clothes and shoes you haven't worn in the last year and add in new items over time to create a new wardrobe.

Create a Confidence Collage

Create a confidence collage with words and pictures to constantly remind yourself of your vision. This is a powerful tool to help you shift your mindset and your life. Take a picture of yourself with your mouth wide open, and then cut out words and images that reflect the positive and empowering things you will now tell yourself whether it be "beautiful, worthy, gorgeous, etc." Also, add in other images that revolve around you becoming the woman you desire to be.

For example, my collage has words such as "wellness, glow, bombshell, shine, work in progress, happy, royalty, love your looks, pamper, have it all, own who you are," and more!

Use my SHIFT acronym to help you put things on your board and consider how all of these things will be present in your life once you become the confident and fierce woman you desire to be:

S- What do you want to see?

H- What do you want to hear? (from others about the confident and empowered you)

I - What or who do you want to be included in your life?

F- How do you want to feel?

T- How do you want to talk to yourself?

Declare Your Desires

You want to claim and declare your desire to be more confident and fierce before you see it manifest in your life. It is called "act as if." Practicing this concept causes your desired results to come quicker.

Examples include the following:

- Create meaningful passwords that affirm you. For example: I love me. I am enough. I am confident and happy.

- Put up meaningful screensavers on phones/ laptops/ Ipads such as your confident collage.

- Customize an empowering laptop or tablet cover that reminds you of your greatness.

- ☐ Buy something that the woman you desire to be would buy. For example, Michael Kors bag, better fitting bras, sexier panties, certain shoes, diamond ring, etc.

- ☐ Put love notes to yourself or post it notes around your bedroom and bathroom or in your purse or car with affirmations written in the present tense.

- ☐ Laminate affirmations and put them in the shower, your bedroom, your home office, your desk at work, etc.

- ☐ Make a confidence playlist and listen to it daily/in the car.

- ☐ Set up automatic reminders on your phone that have "pop up" messages with self-loving words just for you.

Notice that everything suggested is a reflection of what you have the power to do. You want to constantly remind yourself of your power, and the fact that you were #BornFIERCE. Perhaps you already do this. If so, find new ways daily to empower yourself and let this be a reminder that you are on the right path. If not, try one of the ways mentioned in this chapter.

Confidence comes from within. You don't need to search outside of yourself because you can create it day by day on your own terms.

SELFIE CHECK

- What will your daily confidence routine include?
- How will I set up my "empowerment zone?"
- Which confidence boost(s) could enhance my life?

_____

Confidence, happiness, and love come from within me. I believe in myself, and I am committed to my personal growth and development every day. I know that my habits become my character. My character becomes my destiny.

#bornfierce

_____

Download your FREE workbook to complete
the selfie checks at: www.unleashyourfierce.com/fierceworkbook

FINAL FIERCE THOUGHT: STEP INTO YOUR POWER

"The most common way people give up their power is by thinking they don't have any."
- Alice Walker

You have the power! You are officially a member of #FIERCESQUAD. You have the power within you to become all that you were destined to be. No one can make this happen but you. You have been given a very special gift through reading this book. You have been given the gift of wisdom. You have been given the gift of motivation. You have been given the gift of possibility. You have been given the gift of confidence.

Just by reading this book, you are expressing to the universe that you are ready. You are ready to stretch yourself and embark on a beautiful journey that is the journey of being fierce, confident, and unstoppable. You can do it! You have declared what your ideal life looks like, healed the roadblocks standing in the way, and set yourself up for success by committing to building your self-love and confidence every day.

As Martin Luther King Jr. once said, "The journey of a thousand miles starts with a single step." Reading this book is a single step. Life is a continuous journey, and you will cover many steps. My ultimate goal is to help you step into the right direction. Your next step is to step into your personal power by re-reading this book, trying out different exercises and suggestions in this book, speaking affirming words to yourself, and owning the vision you set forth for yourself in the beginning of this book.

As you continue to put one foot in front of the other, you will slowly but surely unleash the confident and fierce woman that has always been within. As you unleash your FIERCE, you will grow and grow and grow until it is turned completely out. Then, you will radiate, and you will SHINE!

Your light will do two things: inspire other women and even younger girls and teens to unleash theirs and shine while it will make others feel totally uncomfortable with who you are becoming. As for that inspiration… Being FIERCE is as much about you as it is about all women who came before you and who will come after.

Do us all a favor, and do as Duke Ellington once said, "Let the whole world benefit from your incredible radiance."

You were born to conquer.

You are beautiful.

You are magnificent.

You are divine.

You are gorgeous.

Own it! Act like it. Walk like it. Talk like it.

Dress like it. Eat like it.

Surround yourself with like-minded people like it.

Move your body like it. Indulge in pleasure like it.

Let it shine, let it shine! You better be FIERCE girl!

As for making others uncomfortable... By committing to this confidence and empowerment journey, you will be seen more and heard more. You will not be able to hide it, if you have been.

People will recognize this new version of you more than ever. Your energy will be contagious. You will be sexier, fiercer, and more fabulous. While most will love the new unleashed you, others may perceive it as "who does she think she is?" So often people get use to us being how we have always been. That will be their issue not yours.

Please don't let it be your own limited thinking that holds you back either. If you have a fear of being perceived as arrogant and conceited then know that is a limited belief you must release. Thinking highly of yourself is not a crime. It is only an issue when you begin to think of yourself better than others and act accordingly. But this is not that type of party because again you will be using your own empowerment to benefit others.

When you shine, you give others permission to shine too! Know that you being in your power means you have to be fearless. Taking it step by step is where the stretching happens. Each time you make a move, the magic happens!

- BORN FIERCE -

Being born fierce mean you were born fiercely and wonderfully. It was no mistake. It was for a reason. It's because you have a calling and because you were sent here to do something of great purpose in this world.

It's about remembering who you are.

In a world of social media self-esteem, media mediocrity, and filtered worthiness it is so easy to forget who you are, why you are here, and what you are here to do.

No matter where you are in your journey; need an extra boost, just had a break up, want to step more into your purpose, ready to become a wife, tired of beating yourself up, need to lose weight, or need to get your sh*t together...you can use the simple #BornFIERCE formula

1. Honor Your Calling

2. Forgive Your Past

3. Fall in Love with Yourself

#BornFIERCE is meant to serve as a reminder, not a wakeup call and not an innovative concept, but just a divine reminder of how damn POWERFUL you are.

You know what to do. You've heard it before. But, this time it will be different.

Women tell me all the time I follow many other coaches who teach similar universal concepts on self-love, confidence, and worthiness. However, they emphasize that the one time they read my work, jumped on a call with me, or got on a webinar with me, it finally clicked.

#BornFIERCE is meant to click for you! If you're reading this book, then you are ready to receive the message--Finally!

If you don't remember anything else, embrace these three #FIERCEISMS:

- When you honor the call, God will make sure you never fall

- When you forgive the past, negativity will never last

- When you fall in love with you, there's nothing that you can't do

At this point, you should have a journal filled that sparked within you "aha" moments, breakthroughs, and ways to transform your life. If not, then be sure to go back through and respond to the selfie checks and suggested exercises to see what works best for upgrading your life to be filled with more love and empowerment.

If there are any parts of this book that have touched you, please get a snapshot of it, repost a piece that resonated with you onto social media, and share with others using the hashtag #bornfierce.

It is imperative that you pay it forward and uplift another woman. We need more women in this world who know that they were born FIERCE, and can confidently operate within their God-given power.

Now…go show them how it's done!

- BORN FIERCE -

Share your favorite quotables, snippets, and aha moments using the hashtag #bornfierce

___

I was born FIERCE!
The confident and fierce woman in me is free
to be unleashed!

#bornfierce

___

− PART IV −
∞
Exclusive Empowerment Extras

BOOK BONUSES

Unleash your FIERCE some more by downloading your FREE bonuses:
www.unleashyourfierce.com/bookbonus
Password: FIERCESQUAD

BOOK CLUB GUIDE

*F*IERCE is an excellent book to read with other women as it is the perfect piece to ignite discussion on a variety of topics that effect modern women every day.

Below you will find a number of discussion questions meant to spark engaging dialogue amongst two or more women.

1. Discuss the significance of the title and concept of the word "fierce". Why do you think it was selected? How is the idea of "fierce" used throughout the book? What women in your own life are "fierce", and what effect did or does it have it on you?

2. What can you take away from Taria's personal journey to evolving as a woman? What is the catalyst for you wanting to evolve and glow? Why do you feel it is now your time to shine?

3. What is your truth? How did it feel to acknowledge it? Why do you think it's important for women to get "real" about who they really are?

4. What "aha" moments or connections did you make when reflecting on your childhood and your mother and father? Why do you think it is good for women to reflect and heal this part of them self?

5. What are your main takeaways from this book in terms of self-love and confidence? What tips and tools will you implement and try in your own life?

6. How do you plan to step into your own personal power as a woman? What are your next steps for becoming the woman you desire to be?

7. What do you now know or understand better that you didn't before reading this book? What parts of this book would you share with other women? Why?

APPENDIX OF AFFIRMATIONS

Daily Self-Love Affirmation

I am forcefully magnetic to the confidence that is divinely housed within me. I am already healed and whole. I am the love of my life. The love that lives inside of me is showing up on the visible plane on a daily basis. My cup is so full that it overflows to others. I live an amazing life! I have been awakened to the confident and fierce woman within me. God is in me, and I know for sure I simply cannot fail.

Other Affirmations
(Use them as you see fit. Add to stickie notes, post cards, posters, vision boards, etc. Most effective when said daily for at least 21 days.)

I am happy, healthy, healed, and whole.

I am a fearless and free. I am admirable, desirable, and a joy to be around.

I light up every room I walk in.

I am valuable and worthy.

I am in love with [insert your name]. She is my Queen and I treasure her.

I am sexy, beautiful, and brilliant.

I am love. I am loved. I am loveable, and I am loving. I love myself completely and give love to each person I meet and interact with.

I glow with feminine power, radiance, mystique, and magnetism.

I am strong on the inside and soft on the outside. I radiate love and light.

I deserve and I surrender to being loved, honored, cherished, and valued.

I honor and love myself just as I am.

I look, speak, and walk with confidence, poise, and power.

I love, honor, and care for my body knowing that it houses the spirit of God, and is a temple of love and life.

I am a woman of high value and virtue who is sought after and stands out from the rest. I always honor my values and my vision.

I am safe, secure, and sure because I know God has me in the palm of his hand. I simply cannot fail. He is never late and is always right on time.

I surrender to divine flow. Love, prosperity, and joy are abundant in my life.

I am attracting the people, circumstances, and finances to make my dreams come true.

I surrender it to God.

I trust everything is working in my favor.

I allow it to unfold divinely.

I am open to receive.

ADDITIONAL RESOURCES

If you are truly ready for a transformational experience then you should check out the following resources available at: www.unleashyourfierce.com:

Unleash Your FIERCE Squad

This private Facebook group is a safe and sacred space to connect with other like-minded women on the Born FIERCE journey. Daily this group is bursting with excitement from videos from Taria, to inspirational tips, and interactive posts to keep you motivated.

Born FIERCE Bootcamp

Born FIERCE Bootcamp is a 21 day holistic journey of mental, physical, spiritual, and emotional elevation. It incorporates elements from this book, and helps you put them in to action consistently. It is perfect to complete the boot camp during or after reading this book.

Unleash Your FIERCE Coaching Program

Unleash Your Fierce is a six-week online coaching experience that will help you step fully into your power and become a stronger, more confident, AND more powerful woman. In six weeks you will learn how to unleash your FIERCE: Find your

FIERCE edge, Ignite your inner Queen, Elevate your confidence, raise men and money magnetism, cultivate your sexiness, and empower yourself daily using proven strategies and techniques for empowered living.

Magnetic with Men Bootcamp

Magnetic with Men Bootcamp is a 21 day online program that allows women to interrupt their old patterns with men, change their inner vibration, and elevate their magnetism as it pertains to dating. The program includes daily audios and four masterclasses on preparing to be a wife, communicating with men, and how to stop attracting the wrong men. This is the perfect program to complete after implementing the principles of Born FIERCE into your life and engaging in deep inner healing work.

Private Coaching

Work with me one-on-one for several months to truly unleash the confident woman within.

ABOUT THE AUTHOR

Taria Pritchett, millennial empowerment powerhouse is a confidence coach for women who want to get their shit together by owning their worth, attracting the right men, and stepping into their purpose.

Selected as one of Delaware's Top 40 under 40 and recently featured in the Huffington Post; she is on a mission to empower women to ditch "bootleg happiness," in favor of becoming their most authentic, happy, FIERCE, and successful selves.

www.ingramcontent.com/pod-product-compliance
Lightning Source LLC
Chambersburg PA
CBHW071129090426
42736CB00012B/2072